SPLINTER

BIDS

Barbara Seagram & Linda Lee

MASTER POINT PRESS • TORONTO

PRACTICE YOUR BIDDING

The PRACTICE YOUR BIDDING Series

Jacoby 2NT
Roman Keycard Blackwood
Splinter Bids
Practice Your Slam Bidding (CD-ROM)

Master Point Press
331 Douglas Avenue
Toronto, Ontario, Canada
M5M 1H2

(416) 781-0351   Internet: **www.masterpointpress.com**

National Library of Canada Cataloguing in Publication

Seagram, Barbara
        Splinter bids / Barbara Seagram & Linda Lee.

(Practice your bidding)
ISBN 1-894154-63-0

1. Contract bridge--Bidding. I. Lee, Linda (Linda Marcia), 1947- II. Title. III. Series.

GV1282.4.S4198 2003   795.41'52   C2003-902594-2

Design and layout: Olena S. Sullivan/New Mediatrix
Editor: Ray Lee

Printed and bound in Canada by Webcom Limited

1 2 3 4 5 6 7   09 08 07 06 05 04 03

TABLE OF CONTENTS

SECTION 1   1
How to Use This Book

SECTION 2   3
How Splinter Bids Work

SECTION 3   15
Working Alone (questions)

SECTION 4   25
Working Alone (answers)

SECTION 5   37
Sample Auctions

SECTION 6   51
Practice Hands

HOW TO USE THIS BOOK

The purpose of this book is to help you and your partner practice Splinter Bids and better understand how they are used. The book has been designed so it can be used either on your own or working with a partner. But while you will certainly get a lot out of it if you use it alone, it is especially good to use this book with your favorite partner to make sure that you are both on the same wavelength.

The first section of the book provides a refresher for the Splinter Bid convention. It provides examples but no exercises. Since cuebids are such an essential part of slam bidding we have also included a refresher on cuebidding. These parts of the book provide lots of examples but no exercises. Don't worry; you will get plenty of chance to practice in the rest of the book. You will also need to ask partner about aces and kings, from time to time. In our sample auctions for demonstration purposes we will use Roman Keycard Blackwood (which is explained in detail in another book in this series). But when you bid the hand, just use your own favorite form of Blackwood. For more explanations, and as a source of many other helpful conventions, you can also refer to *25 Bridge Conventions You Should Know*, by Barbara Seagram and Marc Smith. Check the sections on Cuebids, Blackwood, Roman Keycard Blackwood and Splinter Bids to get the full story.

The last section of the book, 'Practice Hands', contains a set of forty pairs of North and South hands. You can cut them out or copy them and use them with a partner to practice bidding (don't try to do more than about ten at one sitting — that's more than enough to think and talk about at one time). We have provided space beside each hand to write down your auction; we suggest that you do this so you can refer to it when you are looking at the answers. You can also do this solo if you like: look at each hand in turn and write down the bid you would make at each step of the auction. Getting to the right spot is not the only goal; bidding the hand in the best way is another goal so, even if you see both hands, you will still need to work out the correct auction. When you have finished bidding the hands, look at the sample auctions and final contracts provided in the answer section. This book uses Standard American bidding in the sample auctions. There may be more than one way to bid the hand, so don't worry if you don't duplicate our sequence exactly. Focus in particular on your use of Splinter Bids and make sure that you get that right.

There is an earlier section of the book, entitled 'Working Alone' which contains the same practice deals. In this section, we show you just one of the hands and ask you a series of questions about how to bid it as the auction develops. Working through these exercises will teach you a lot more about the convention, so even if you go through the practice deals with a partner, we suggest you go through the questions and try to answer them. This will help you to make sure that you understand the convention thoroughly.

A final warning: don't expect to be perfect. Some of these hands are hard. So if you are doing better at the end of the book then at the beginning, you are doing very well indeed.

What are splinters?

Splinter bids are special raises of partner's suit. They are a way of supporting partner and also providing a very specific message about your hand. The message is that you have the following:

1) at least 4-card trump support for partner;
2) a singleton or void in a side suit (this is the 'splinter suit');
3) you have a hand with enough support points to make game — so if you are splintering over partner's major-suit opening bid you have 13-15 dummy points — never more than 15.

We make the meaning of a splinter bid so specific because, as you will see, a splinter takes up a lot of bidding space. When you make this bid you need to tell partner a lot because partner will not have much bidding room to ask more questions afterwards.

When you splinter it is clear that you plan to play the hand in game in partner's suit since your side has enough points for game. So splinters are a way of looking for slam. It's possible you'll be able to make a slam on high-card power when your partner has a very strong hand, but most of the time you are looking for a slam based on fit. You are hoping that this time there will be some magic which will allow you to make a slam on fewer than the normal 33 points.

How do you splinter?

A splinter bid is a double jump in a new suit.
Here are two examples of splinter bids:

Partner	You	Partner	You
1♠	4♢	1♡	3♠

In the first auction, your 4◇ bid shows a singleton or void in diamonds, four-card support for partner's spades and 13-15 points in support of spades. In the second auction, your 3♠ bid shows a singleton or void in spades and a game raise in hearts.

Your bids in these two auctions are not splinters:

Partner	You	Partner	You
1♠	3◇	1♡	2♣

The first bid is a jump shift showing a very strong hand with a diamond suit. The second bid is a normal response in clubs, showing clubs and forcing for one round. Notice that neither of these bids promises support for partner's suit.

There are two common types of splinter bids and we will review each of these types separately. The first type is made by responder after an opening bid. The second occurs when opener makes a splinter bid in support of responder's suit. Let's look at each of these.

Splinters by responder

The most common splinter bids by responder occur over a major-suit opening bid.

Let's look at some examples of hands and decide if they are suitable for a splinter bid over a major-suit opening. In all cases partner has opened with 1♠:

    a) ♠ K 9 8 3 ♡ A K 9 3 2 ◇ 4 ♣ Q 10 3
    b) ♠ K Q 8 3 ♡ A Q 5 4 ◇ A K 3 2 ♣ 7
    c) ♠ A K 3 ♡ 7 ◇ K 7 5 4 3 ♣ K 9 8 2
    d) ♠ J 10 5 4 ♡ K 7 6 2 ◇ 5 ♣ Q 7 6 3
    e) ♠ A J 6 2 ♡ — ◇ K Q 10 7 2 ♣ 7 6 3 2

With hand (a) you would bid 4◇ (splinter) since you meet all of the qualifications. With hand (b) you are too strong for a splinter bid. You should use Jacoby 2NT if you are playing that convention. With hand (c) you do not have four-card trump support and you should therefore bid 2◇ for now; you will raise spades later in the auction. With hand (d) you are too weak to splinter and you should simply bid 2♠. Hand (e) is another excellent one for a splinter bid and you should bid 4♡. Notice that a splinter bid can show either a singleton or a void.

It is very rare to use a splinter bid over opener's minor-suit opening bid. Why is that? If partner opens one of a major and you discover a nine-card fit, you will almost always want to play in that suit. However, when partner opens one of a minor you are often not yet sure where you want to play the hand, even if you have a fit for partner's minor. If you have a four-card major you may still end up playing in that suit, since partner could still have a four-card fit for you; similarly, you may want to play in 3NT instead of five of a minor if you have stoppers in the side suits. In addition, partner may only have three or four cards in his minor suit so you need to have at least a five-card fit to make a splinter bid a good choice. If you are going to splinter over a minor you will need 16-18 points since you are showing values for game; remember, game in the minor is at the five-level, and you will require about 29 points between your two hands.

Splinters by opener

When responder bids a new suit, opener can also make a splinter bid with a singleton or void in a side suit and enough points to commit the partnership to game. If responder bids at the one level opener needs 19–21 dummy points to splinter since responder has only promised 6 points.

A splinter by opener shows:

1) four-card (or more) support;
2) a singleton or void in the splinter suit;
3) enough points to make game.

Here are two examples of splinters by opener:

Opener	Responder	Opener	Responder
1 ◊	1 ♡	1 ♡	1 ♠
4 ♣		4 ♣	

In both examples opener is showing a singleton or void in clubs and 19 to 21 dummy points. In the first example opener is showing a four-card or better heart raise and in the second example a four-card or better spade raise.

There is one other case and it is a little more complicated. It comes up when responder's first bid was at the two-level. For example, opener holds

♠ K 9 8 5 2 ♡ A K 9 3 2 ◊ 3 ♣ A 10

and the auction has proceeded:

You	Partner
1♠	2♡
?	

As opener you know that you want to play in 4♡, and possibly in slam. You could just bid 4♡, but slam is possible if partner has a good fitting hand. What do you bid? It would seem that you would have to bid 5◊ to splinter in support of hearts (a double jump). However in this auction, a 3◊ rebid by you is forcing to game and shows extra values, so you do not need 4◊ as a strong jump shift. Therefore, as an exception, *a single jump bid by opener is a splinter bid if the double jump would take you higher than the four-level.*

Opener can splinter over partner's minor-suit response on occasion. This will normally happen when opener has a very distributional hand and has ruled out notrump. For example, you hold

♠ A 10 9 5 4 ♡ A 3 ◊ A Q J 10 5 ♣ 7

and the auction has proceeded:

You	Partner
1♠	2◊
?	

With this highly distributional hand you do not want to play this hand in notrump. The best bid is 4♣, a splinter bid. Notice that you have bypassed 3NT and are now committed to playing this hand in a suit contract, likely in diamonds (or just possibly spades if partner has three-card support).

Can you splinter with a singleton ace or king?

When you make a splinter bid, partner will devalue any high cards that he holds in your short suit (and upgrade high cards in other suits). If you have a king or ace in the short suit partner is going to get the wrong idea about the value of honors in the short suit that he may hold. Therefore you should not splinter with a singleton ace or king. This agreement will allow partner to make a good decision about whether to make a move towards slam. For example, if partner holds the king and queen in clubs and you splinter in clubs he will assume these high cards are wasted. However, if you actually have the singleton ace, his king and queen might be quite valuable. Since your hand is limited partner will also assume that the high cards that you do have are in your long suits and not in your short suits and this will allow him to determine the quality of the fit and decide whether to continue.

Reevaluating your hand after a splinter bid

When partner makes a splinter bid, it's time to re-evaluate your hand. Your hand gets better if you have little or no values in partner's short suit and worse if you have high cards in partner's short suit. Kings, queens and jacks in partner's short suit are usually wasted. The exception is that an ace in the short suit will still be useful if partner has a singleton. Lets look at some examples.

You open 1♡ and partner splinters in diamonds:

You	Partner
1♡	4◇
?	

a)	♠ K 9 3	b)	♠ K 9 3
	♡ A K 7 3 2		♡ A K 7 3 2
	◇ 10 9 3		◇ K J 3
	♣ K J		♣ 10 9

Hand (a) and (b) are the same except that we have switched the club honors to diamonds. Hand (b) has worsened because your diamond high cards are wasted. Hand (a) has improved because you have no wasted cards in diamonds. Let us look at an example hand from partner and see why this is.

	You	Partner
a)	♠ K 9 3	♠ A Q 6 4
	♡ A K 7 3 2	♡ Q 10 5 4
	◇ 10 9 3	◇ 4
	♣ K J	♣ A 8 5 2

If you have hand (a) your side can make exactly 6♡ with one diamond loser. Of course, these hands are exceptionally easy to bid to game because you have 26 H.C.P. between the two hands. What you are really trying to do is get to a slam on only 26 points — you are looking for magic, which is what having only small cards opposite partner's singleton means. (Another holding that should turn you on is Axx, where you have the ace and no other high cards opposite partner's singleton.) When partner has a singleton, six of the opponents' high card points in that suit (the king, queen and jack) will not win a trick. It is as though you are playing with a 34-point deck. As a result, you need fewer high cards to make slam.

	You	**Partner**
b)	♠ K 9 3	♠ A Q 6 4
	♡ A K 7 3 2	♡ Q 10 5 4
	◇ K J 3	◇ 4
	♣ 10 9	♣ A 8 5 2

Here you have the king and jack of diamonds opposite partner's singleton. Suppose you lead a small diamond from dummy and play the ◇J from your hand. It loses to the ◇Q and now you have to trump both the ◇K and the ◇3. Alas, 4 of your 26 points just got thrown out the window. None of those cards won tricks in their own right; you had to trump them, so they may as well have been the ◇432 for all the good they did you. You probably still have to lose a club (since spades will likely not divide 3-3). There's no magic here — just wasted high cards opposite partner's shortness, and probably no slam either.

Opener's rebids after responder splinters

When partner makes a splinter bid, you know that he has 13-15 points including distribution. You will need about 18 points in your hand to make a slam. However, you can make a slam try if your hand has improved and you have at least 16 points including distribution. If you have 19 points or more you should make a slam try even if your hand has not been improved by partner's bid.

Let's look at some examples after you open 1♠ and partner splinters in clubs

a) ♠ A K 8 7 3	b) ♠ A J 10 6 3	c) ♠ A K J 10 9
♡ K J 9 8	♡ K 9 8 2	♡ A Q 3
◇ A 3	◇ K 2	◇ Q 6 5
♣ 3 2	♣ K J	♣ K 2

You	**Partner**
1♠	4♣
?	

With hand (a) you should make a slam try; you have 16+ points including distribution and you have no club wastage. You should not make a slam try with hand (b) because although you have enough points, you have wasted club values. With hand (c) you should make a slam try. Although you have wasted club values you do have a very strong hand, with enough for slam anyway.

Responder's rebids after opener splinters

When partner splinters over your one-level response you know that he has at least 19 support points, four trumps and shortness in the splinter suit. In order to justify a slam try, you will need at least 10 points including distribution if your hand has improved and at least 13 points if your hand has not improved. Here is an example of a 10-point hand that is worth a slam try after partner has opened 1◇ and splintered to 4♣ over your 1♡ response.

Partner	You
1◇	1♡
4♣	

♠ K 8 7　♡ K 10 9 4 3　◇ K J　♣ 7 6 2

Even though it doesn't look like much, this hand is a powerhouse opposite partner's expected hand. Remember, partner has a singleton or void in clubs, and all his high cards are in the other three suits. Partner might have

Partner	You
♠ A J 3	♠ K 8 7
♡ A Q J 6	♡ K 10 9 4 3
◇ A Q 9 8 7	◇ K J
♣ 3	♣ 7 6 2

If you look at these two hands, you'll see that 6♡ is an excellent spot. Here is an example of a hand that would make a slam try in the same auction despite a poor fit (because you have so many points):

Partner	You
1◇	1♡
4♣	

♠ K 8 7　♡ K 10 9 4 3　◇ K 2　♣ K J 2

Again, if partner has the same hand:

Partner	You
♠ A J 3	♠ K 8 7
♡ A Q J 6	♡ K 10 9 4 3
◇ A Q 9 8 7	◇ K 2
♣ 3	♣ K J 2

you can still make slam even though you have wasted club values.

Continuing the auction after a splinter

If after re-evaluating your hand, you decide you do not have enough to make a slam try that would take the auction past game, then bid four of the agreed major. This bid is a 'sign-off'. It tells partner that you do not want to proceed past game. If you do have enough extra values to move forward, you can either cuebid or use Blackwood.

Suppose that after partner splinters you are sure that slam is there if partner has enough controls (aces and trump honors). In this situation it might be a good time to use Blackwood or Roman Keycard Blackwood. Remember that you might want to explore for grand slam so don't just jump to Blackwood if you need more information to make that decision. Here is an example of a hand where Blackwood would be appropriate.

♠ K Q J 9 8 3 ♡ K Q 9 3 ◇ A 4 ♣ A

You	Partner
1♠	4◇
?	

Bid 4NT. If partner has two aces then you want to be in a grand slam and if partner has only one ace then small slam is fine.

If you want to test the waters and find out more about partner's hand then the best approach is to make a cuebid. Since you have agreed on the trump suit , any suit other than the trump suit that you bid is a cuebid. The section below describes cuebids and how to use them.

Some unusual splinters

This section is for those who wish to be more adventurous in their use of splinters. It is quite alright to skip this section if you don't yet want to try something that can be a bit complex.

There are other situations where you may wish to use a splinter, as well as the common ones we have looked at so far. For example, you may wish to splinter in a competitive auction after partner makes an overcall, or you may wish to splinter in the later stages of a constructive auction. The requirements are still the same, at least four-card trump support, enough points to be sure that your side should be in game, and a singleton or void in a side suit. Here are some examples:

a)	**Oppt.**	**Partner**	**Oppt.**	**Partner**
	1◇	1♠	pass	4♣

a)	**Oppt.**	**Partner**	**Oppt.**	**Partner**
			1♡	dbl
	pass	2♠	pass	4♣

In example (a), 4♣ is a splinter bid in support of partner's overcall. The requirements are very similar to the requirements for a splinter when partner opens the bidding 1♠. However, since partner does not have to have an opening bid to overcall, you should have 16-18 dummy points to force to game. In example (b), partner has made a jump response of 2♠ to your takeout double, thereby showing 8–10 points and at least four spades. The 4♣ splinter bid is similar to the type that you would make if partner had responded 1♠ after you had opened the bidding.

c)	**Partner**	**You**
	1◇	1♡
	2◇	4♣

d)	**Partner**	**You**
	1♣	1♡
	1♠	4◇

e)	**Partner**	**You**
	1◇	1♠
	2♠	4♣

These three auctions are examples of splinter bids that you might make later in the auction. In auction (c), you wanted to bid your major suit first before supporting partner's diamonds. Once partner does not raise hearts, you decide that diamonds is the best spot. In auction (d), you splinter in support of partner's second suit. In auction (e), you 'self-splinter', in support of your own spades.

One thing to remember, if you are going to add these special splinters to your repertoire, is that at this stage of the auction you have some additional information about partner's values. A splinter is a slam try. There is no point in making a slam try if you know that your side has no chance for slam. So you do need to have enough values to know that slam is possible if partner has a good fitting hand. In auction (e) it would not be worth using a splinter bid on a minimum thirteen-point hand, even if you had a singleton. Partner's hand is limited by his 2♠ bid. You should have a hand that is worth 16-18 points in spades to use a splinter bid.

A Review of Cuebids

A cuebid is a bid made to show a first- or second-round control in a suit. Having a 'control' means that you can stop the opponents from taking too many winners in that suit by winning the trick yourself. Here are examples of controls in the spade suit when hearts are trumps:

a) ♠ A 3 2
b) ♠ —
c) ♠ K 5
d) ♠ 6

Examples (a) and (b) show first-round spade control: if spades are led you will be able to take the first trick. In example (a) you will win the ace and in example (b) you will trump the spade. Examples (c) and (d) show a second-round control in spades: if the opponents lead spades you will be able to take the second trick. Note that there is some risk with example (c) if the spade is led through the ♠K (assuming partner does not have the ♠Q), but this still counts as a control.

Sometimes we use cuebids on our way to slam. This is often the case when we have a hand that is unsuitable for Blackwood, either because we have two or three small in a side suit, or because the hand contains a void. We will use them both to indicate slam interest and to show partner that we have a control in a suit.

In order to make a slam, your side must have controls in all of the side suits. Here is an example of a hand with many tricks but where you can't make slam:

Partner	You
♠ A J 5 4 3	♠ K Q 10 9 7
♡ 5 4	♡ 9 2
◇ K Q J 10 9	◇ A
♣ A	♣ K Q J 10 9

These hands have fifteen top tricks. Unfortunately the opponents have the first two hearts so slam cannot be made! Your side does not have a heart control.

When is a bid a cuebid?

How do you know if a bid of a new suit is a cuebid? In a splinter auction, after the splinter any suit bid other than the trump suit is a cuebid because your side has agreed on a trump suit:

Partner	You	Partner	You	Partner	You
1♠	4◇	1♡	4♣	1◇	1♡
4♡		5♣		4♣	4◇

In the first auction 4♡ is a cuebid showing a first round-heart control. In the second auction hand 5♣ is a cuebid showing a first-round club control. In the third auction 4◇ is a cuebid showing a first-round diamond control.

What suit should you cuebid?

What suit should you cuebid? You start by bidding first-round controls first, and you bid your cheapest first round control first. 'Cheapest' means that you bid the next one up the line in the auction. The advantage of this is that when you bypass a side suit you deny having the first-round control in that suit. Later, you bid your second-round controls as cheaply as possible.

Note that we never cuebid first- or second-round control in the trump suit.
Here are some examples:

You	Partner
1♡	3♠
?	

In this auction clubs is the 'cheapest' cuebid, diamonds second and hearts last.

You hold:

a) ♠ 5 4 ♡ A Q J 4 3 2 ◇ A K J ♣ A 2
b) ♠ 5 4 ♡ A K 10 4 3 2 ◇ A 2 ♣ K Q J
c) ♠ A 2 ♡ A K J 7 4 3 ◇ 5 4 ♣ A K J

With Hand (a) bid 4♣. This shows a first-round club control.
With Hand (b) bid 4◇. This shows a first-round diamond control
        and denies a first-round control in clubs.
With Hand (c) bid 4♣. If partner can bid 4◇, you will be headed for
        slam.

Here is an example of a hand where you use cuebidding to get to a slam:

Partner	You
♠ Q J	♠ A 3
♡ A Q J 9	♡ K 10 5 4
◇ 9	◇ 8 7 3 2
♣ A K 10 5 3	♣ Q J 8
1♣	1♡
4◇¹	4♠²
4NT	5♡³
6♡	

1. Splinter
2. Cuebid
3. 2 keycards, no trump Q

When partner splinters in diamonds, your hand is worth a slam try. You cuebid showing your ♠A and your partner can bid Blackwood once he knows that you have a first-round spade control. Your side reaches slam.

Deal 1

♠ A Q J 4 2
♡ J 4
◇ K Q 9
♣ J 8 7

You open the bidding 1♠ and partner responds 4◇.

1. What does partner's 4◇ bid show?
2. Has this bid improved your hand?
3. What should you do now?

Deal 2

♠ Q 10 7 4
♡ K J 8 6
◇ K Q 5 3
♣ 7

1. Partner has opened the bidding 1♡; what is your best response?
2. What would be your best response if partner opened the bidding with 1♠?
3. What if partner opened the bidding 1◇, what would you bid?

Deal 3

♠ J 10 8 7 5
♡ A Q J
◇ K 2
♣ J 5 4

1. Partner has opened the hand with 1♠. What should you bid?
2. Suppose the auction has proceeded as follows

Partner	You
1◇	1♠
4♣	?

a) What does partner's 4♣ bid show?
b) What should you bid now?

Deal 4

♠ Q 7 6 4
♡ 4
♢ K 7 6 5 2
♣ Q J 5

1. Partner opens 1♠. What is your best response?
2. What would you do next in this auction?

Partner	You
1♡	1♠
4♣	?

Deal 5

♠ 8
♡ K 7 3 2
♢ K J 9 8
♣ K Q 7 6

1. Partner opens 1♡ and you decide to splinter. Is this the correct bid, and why?
2. If partner rebids 4♣ or 4♢ over your splinter, what do these bids mean?

Deal 6

♠ K Q 8 3 2
♡ A 9 8 4
♢ K Q 3
♣ 7

The auction has gone

You	Partner
1♠	2♡
?	

1. You have decided to splinter in clubs. How do you splinter in this situation?
2. Would you splinter in clubs if partner had responded 2♢ instead?

Deal 7 - Dealer South

SOUTH
♠ Q 9 8
♡ K Q J 7 5
♢ A J 2
♣ J 5

1. You open 1♡ and partner splinters with one of the following bids. Has your hand improved? What would you do next in each case?
   a) 3♠
   b) 4♣

Deal 8

♠ A Q J 10
♡ 6 5 4
♢ 7
♣ K Q 10 4 2

1. You are pleased to hear partner open the bidding with 1♠. Should you splinter on this hand and why?
2. If partner opened with 1♣, what would you bid?

Deal 9

♠ Q 10 9 8 3
♡ A K J 4 2
◇ 3
♣ K 5

The auction has started

You	Partner
1♠	2♡

1. You decide to splinter. What do you bid and why?
2. If you splinter with 4◇ and partner now bids 4♡, what should you do?

Deal 10

♠ 3
♡ K Q 8 7
◇ A K J 8 5
♣ K J 3

The auction has started:

You	Partner
1◇	1♡

1. Should you splinter into spades?
2. Suppose that you bid 3♠ and partner makes the following responses. What should you do in each case?
   a) 4♡   b) 4♣   c) 6♡

Deal 11

♠ A K Q 3
♡ J 9 7 5
◇ 3
♣ A K 6 5

1. What do you bid if partner makes the following opening bids:
   a) 1♠   b) 1◇
2. The auction has gone:

Partner	You
1◇	1♡
1♠	?

Should you splinter now?

Deal 12

♠ 4
♡ A J 6 3
◇ A K Q
♣ K 10 6 5 2

1. You open the hand with 1♣ and partner bids 1♡. Do you have the right hand to splinter, and why?
2. The auction has gone

Partner	You
	1♣
1♡	3♠
4♣	?

What should you bid now?

Deal 13

♠ A Q 9 8 5
♡ K J 7
◇ K 7 3 2
♣ 4

1. You open the hand 1♠ and partner makes one of the following bids. What would you do next in each case?
   a) 4◇
   b) 4♡
   c) 2◇

Deal 14

♠ K J 10 9 8
♡ 3
◇ Q J 8 5 2
♣ A Q

1. If partner splinters in diamonds over your 1♠ opening bid, what should you do?
2. Partner bids 2◇ over your 1♠ opening bid. This hand definitely looks like it will play best in a suit. Should you splinter or just raise diamonds? If you decide to splinter, what is the correct bid?

Deal 15

♠ A K J 9 4
♡ K 10 5 4
◇ K 2
♣ 5 4

1. You open 1♠ and partner bids 2◇. What should you bid now?
2. The auction has gone

You	Partner
1♠	2◇
2♡	4♣

What does partner's 4♣ mean?
3. What should you bid over partner's 4♣ bid?

Deal 16

♠ K 10 5 4
♡ A K 7 2
◇ 6
♣ K Q 5 2

1. Partner opens the hand with 1♣. Should you splinter and why?
2. The auction has gone as follows. What should you do next?

Partner	You
1♣	1♡
2♡	?

Deal 17

♠ A K J 5 4
♡ K J 9
◇ A Q 7 6
♣ 7

1. You open this hand 1♠. What would you do if partner made each of the following responses:
   a) 4♠   b) 4◇   c) 4♡

Deal 18

♠ 6
♡ A K Q 7
◇ K Q 10 5 4
♣ A Q 3

1. Your partner opens 1♡. Should you splinter?
2. Where do you expect to play this hand? What do you need to know to make the final decision?

Deal 19

♠ A K J 10 6
♡ 8 2
◇ A Q J 10 2
♣ A

1. Partner opens 1♠. You can't splinter to show the singleton club and trump support for two reasons. What are they?
2. Slam seems likely. What should you bid over the 1♠ opening?

Deal 20

♠ A J 3
♡ A J 9 8 5
◇ K Q J 9 2
♣ —

The auction has gone:

You	Partner
1♡	2◇
?	

1. What would you do now and why?
2. If you decide to splinter in clubs, and partner bids 5◇ next, what should you do?

Deal 21

♠ A 9 6
♡ K Q 8 7 6 5
◇ 3
♣ A K 9

1. Partner opens 1♠. Should you splinter?
2. The auction has gone:

You	Partner
	1♠
2♡	4♣

   a) What does partner's 4♣ bid mean ?
   b) What should you do over partner's 4♣ bid?

Deal 22

♠ A
♡ K 10 9 8 7
♦ K Q 5 4 3
♣ 7 6

1. Partner opens 1♦. Should you splinter?
2. Should you splinter if partner opens 1♡?

Deal 23

♠ A Q J 3 2
♡ A Q
♦ 10 9 8 5 3
♣ 6

1. If partner opens 1♦ what would you respond?
2. The auction has proceeded as follows:

Partner	You
1♡	1♠
2♦	?

What is your next bid?
3. If partner makes a slam try after you agree diamonds, what would you do then?

Deal 24

♠ K 9 6 4 3
♡ Q 10 9
♦ —
♣ A J 10 8 3

1. What would you bid if partner opened 1♡?
2. What would you bid if partner opened 1♠?
3. What about responding to a 1♣ opener?
4. If partner opens 1♠ and you splinter, have you
shown the void?

Deal 25

♠ K Q 2
♡ A Q
♦ A 9 8 7 6 5 4
♣ 6

1. Partner opens 1♦. Should you splinter and why?
2. What do you need for slam?

Deal 26

♠ K 10 9 3 2
♡ A Q
♦ A J 6
♣ J 7 6

1. The auction has proceeded:

Partner	You
1♣	1♠
4♦	?

What does partner have for his 4♦ bid?
2. What should you do now?

Deal 27

♠ K Q 9 5 4
♡ A 5 4 3
◇ K J 10
♣ 10

1. You open 1♠. What would you bid over the following responses from partner?
   a) 4◇
   b) 4♡
   c) 3♠ (limit raise)

Deal 28

♠ A K J 5 2
♡ A Q 10
◇ J 4 3 2
♣ 9

1. You open 1♠. Would you splinter if partner responded 2♡?
2. Partner splinters with 4◇ over your 1♠ opening. What should you do now?

Deal 29

♠ A K Q
♡ 9
◇ A J 10 5 4
♣ A 6 5 2

1. Partner opens 1♠. Should you splinter?
2. Should you play this hand in diamonds or spades if partner raises diamonds?
3. If the auction goes this way, what do you know about partner's hand and what should you do next?

You	Partner
	1♠
2◇	3◇

Deal 30

♠ Q 9 8 6
♡ 3
◇ K Q J 9 5
♣ K 8 4

1. Partner opens 1♠. Should you splinter on this hand?
2. What would you bid if partner opened 1◇?

Deal 31

♠ Q
♡ K Q J 5 2
◇ A J 7
♣ K Q J 3

1. You open 1♡ and partner bids 4♣, what would you do?
2. Suppose your partner bid 4◇ instead?

Deal 32

♠ 9 8 7 6 5 4
♡ 3
◇ K Q 5 4 3
♣ 3

1. Partner opens 1 spade. What bid should you make and why?
2. What would you do if partner had opened 1◇?

Deal 33

♠ 9 8 7
♡ A K 4 3 2
◇ 7
♣ Q J 10 2

1. Should you open the bidding as dealer?
2. If you pass as dealer, and partner opens 1♡, what is your best response?
3. What would you bid if partner had opened 1♠?

Deal 34

♠ A 9 8 5
♡ A Q 6
◇ 2
♣ A K 8 7 3

1. You open 1♣ and partner bids 1♠. What should you bid now and why?
2. If partner signs off in 4♠, do you have enough to push on to slam anyway?

Deal 35

♠ A 7 5 4
♡ 3
◇ K 4 2
♣ A J 10 7 6

1. Partner overcalls 1♠ after the opponents open 1◇. What should you bid now?
2. If partner had opened the bidding 1♠ rather than overcalling, would you still make the same bid?

Deal 36

♠ K 10 9 5 2
♡ A Q 6 5
◇ Q J 5
♣ 7

1. Partner opens 1♡. What do you bid?
2. What would you do over a 1♠ opening bid?
3. Suppose the auction has proceeded as follows

Partner	You
1♡	4♣
4♠	

What does 4♠ show, and what do you do?

Deal 37

♠ K 2
♡ K Q 8 5 4
◇ 6
♣ A K J 5 4

1. Partner opens 1♣. Should you splinter?
2. If the auction goes as follows, should you splinter now?

Partner	You
1♣	1♡
2♣	?

Deal 38

♠ A Q 9 8 5
♡ K Q 9
◇ 8 3 2
♣ K 2

1. You open this hand with 1♠. Does your hand get better or worse if partner bids
   a) 4♣
   b) 4◇
   c) 4♡
2. If partner bids 4♡, what should you bid next?

Deal 39

♠ A Q 8 4 3
♡ K Q J 2
◇ 9
♣ K 7 6

1. You open 1♠ and partner bids 2♡. What should you bid now?
2. If the auction goes

Partner	You
	1♠
2♡	4◇
4♠	

What should you bid now?

Deal 40

♠ K Q 10 9 2
♡ 3
◇ A Q 9 8 4
♣ A K

1. Partner has opened 1♠. Should you splinter?
2. The auction has gone

Partner	You
1♡	1♠
2◇	

Should you splinter now? If not, what should you bid?

Deal 1

1. 4◊ is a splinter bid. It shows at least four spades, 13-15 dummy points, and a singleton diamond.
2. No. This bid has made your hand worse. You have wasted diamond points opposite partner's singleton.
3. Bid 4♠. This bid is a signoff and tells partner that you have no slam interest in this auction.

Deal 2

1. Bid 4♣, splinter. You have four trumps, between 13 and 15 dummy points and a singleton club. This hand is an ideal splinter bid.
2. Bid 4♣, splinter. You have four-card trump support for spades as well.
3. Bid 1♡. You would not want to splinter over a minor suit opening on this hand. You are still not sure where you want to play this hand. With two four-card majors you are hoping that partner has a fit for one of them and that you can play in a major suit contract.

Deal 3

1. Bid Jacoby 2NT (or whatever you use to show a game raise in partner's major).
2. a) 4♣ is a splinter. It shows four-card spade support, 19–21 dummy points in spades, and a singleton or void in clubs.
   b) Bid 4NT, Blackwood. You are definitely interested in slam. The splinter bid has improved your hand since you have only

1 wasted point in clubs. You have a hand worth 14 dummy points and partner is known to have 19 – 21 dummy points.

Deal 4

1. Bid 3♠ (limit raise). You do not have a good enough hand to force to game so a splinter is out.
2. Bid 4♠. This is a signoff. You do not have a lot of extra values for your one spade bid, and partner's splinter means that your club honors are wasted. You will probably not take even one club trick with these high cards.

Deal 5

1. Yes, you should splinter. You have four-card trump support, 13-15 dummy points and a singleton spade. You meet the qualifications.
2. Either 4♣ or 4◊ would be a cuebid. Partner is making a slam try. Your splinter has improved partner's hand or partner has a powerhouse and thinks that slam is possible.

Deal 6

1. Bid 4♣. Normally you would need to make a double jump to splinter. This is an exception since a double jump would take you to the five-level.
2. No, you should bid 2♡. You would prefer to play the hand in a major, and partner may still have four hearts. In any case, you need 4-card support to splinter.

Deal 7

1 a) Your hand has not improved since your ♠Q is not pulling its full weight. Since partner has a spade singleton or void your are unlikely to take a single trick with this card. Bid 4♡

  b) Your hand has improved somewhat. Your ♣J is wasted but you were never counting it for much anyway. Cuebid 4◊. This will help your partner if he is worried about a diamond control and suggest slam interest. However you have very little extra so it is now up to partner to push for slam.

Deal 8

1. Bid 4◇. You have four-card trump support. You have between 13 and 15 dummy points. You have a singleton diamond. The splinter describes your hand perfectly.
2. Bid 1♠. You do not know for sure that you want to play in clubs. A major-suit may be the right contract. You can't splinter until you determine the right suit to play in.

Deal 9

1. Bid 4◇. In this auction 4◇ shows a splinter since a double jump would take you past the four-level. What if you had natural diamonds and a good hand? You would just bid 3◇ since this bid creates a game force after partners 2 over 1 response.
2. Pass. You have fully shown your hand. If partner is not interested in slam then you have nothing further to say.

Deal 10

1. Yes, bid 3♠. You have enough to force to game over partner's 1♡ response. Show partner your spade singleton and see if he can proceed to slam.
2. a) Pass. You have already shown partner your hand.
   b) Partner is showing you first-round club control, probably the ♣A, and trying for slam. You are happy to go on to slam, so just use Blackwood.
   c) Pass and wish your partner good luck. Your splinter bid worked -- you have made it to slam.

Deal 11

1. a) Use your favorite game raise convention, such as Jacoby 2NT. Your hand is too good to splinter. A splinter shows 13-15 dummy points and you have a lot more than that.
   b) Bid 1♡. With 17 high card points, you have a good hand and the first job is to find the best fit to play in.
2. No, you cannot splinter into partner's suit. If you bid diamonds you will be raising your partner's suit. Best just to raise to 4♠ now.

Deal 12

1. Yes, bid 3♠, splinter. You have 19 dummy points in hearts. This should be enough to make game opposite partner's response. With four trumps and a singleton spade, you meet the requirements for a splinter.

2. Partner is making a move towards slam and showing a first-round club control, likely the ♣A. You certainly have the values to go on to slam. Bid Blackwood especially if you are playing Roman Keycard Blackwood since this convention allows you to find out about the ♡K and ♡Q. If partner has two aces and the ♡K and ♡Q, you will have five heart tricks, three diamonds, one spade, two clubs and likely two spade ruffs.

Deal 13

1 a) Bid 4♠. You do not have a lot of extra values and your ♢K is not very valuable opposite partner's singleton. It might take one trick if the ♢A is onside (in front of the king) but it is not as useful as high cards in partner's longer suits.

b) Bid 4♠. You have an even worse hand opposite heart shortness. Now the ♡K and ♡J are both wasted.

c) Bid 3♢. You do not have enough to splinter and force to game if partner has a minimum 10 points. In addition, even though you have a singleton, 3NT may be the best game for your side if partner has club values. If you splinter in clubs you will have bypassed 3NT.

Deal 14

1. Bid 4♠. You have wasted diamond values and not much extra.

2. Bid 4♡, splinter. This hand is worth 17 dummy points and should make game opposite your partner's 2♢ bid. You have five trumps and a singleton and therefore the right hand for a splinter.

Deal 15

1. Bid 2♡. Show your second suit.

2. 4♣ is a splinter bid in support of hearts. Partner is showing 13-15 dummy points (enough for game), four hearts and a singleton club.

3. You have more than a minimum opener, and what's more, you know that your hands fit well since you have no wasted club points opposite partner's singleton. You should be able to make slam if you are not missing two aces. Bid 4NT.

Deal 16

1. No. Clubs may not be the best place to play this hand. First, partner may only have a three-card suit. Second, partner may have a four-card major and that would provide an easier contract for game. And finally, even if the club fit is the best one for your side, 3NT might be the right spot since you need only nine tricks and not eleven. We seldom splinter over an opening bid of one of a minor.

2. Bid 4♣. It is not wrong to splinter, but it is possible partner has only three hearts (with a hand like ♠xx ♡QJx ◇AJx ♣Axxxx), and clubs may be the right spot.

Deal 17

1 a) Pass. Although you do have an excellent hand, partner's 4♠ bid is a preempt and you do not expect to make slam.

b) Bid 4NT. Although the ◇Q is wasted you still have a very good hand with lots of extra points. You have 20 points opposite partner's 13, and 33 = the sound of slam! If partner has enough for a spade game opposite a minimum opener, you would expect to make slam most of the time (assuming you are not missing two aces).

c) Bid 4NT. The heart splinter has not improved your hand at all since you now know that the ♡K and ♡J do not have much value. However, your hand is so good that you will likely make slam anyway.

Deal 18

1. No, don't splinter. A splinter promises no more than 13–15 dummy points. You have a lot more than that. You will have to find another bid — 3◇ or 2◇, depending on your style.

2. Bid 4NT. This hand is a powerhouse! You expect to play in six or seven hearts. The only thing you need to know is information about partner's aces. If partner has the two missing aces you can

make grand slam with five heart tricks, one spade trick, four or five diamond tricks, a club trick and one or two spade ruffs.

Deal 19

1. You can't splinter because 1) your singleton is the ace and 2) you have too many points. You do not splinter with a singleton ace or king because partner will expect you to have your high cards in other suits, not the splinter suit.

2. Bid Jacoby 2NT (or an alternative game raise in spades) or jump shift into diamonds and support spades later if you are not playing Jacoby 2 NT. You can't bid Blackwood without a first- or second-round control in hearts.

Deal 20

1. Bid 4♣, a splinter bid. Even though it is only a single jump it is still a splinter because the double jump would take you to the five-level (remember that exception). You have the values to force to game in diamonds, five-card trump support and a void in clubs.

2. Pass. You have described your hand. Partner probably has wasted club cards.

Deal 21

1. No, you should not splinter without four-card trump support. Bid 2♡.

2. a) Partner's 4♣ bid is a splinter. Partner has at most one club, four hearts and enough for game (16-18 dummy points).

   b) Although your club cards are opposite partner's singleton or void, you have an excellent hand. Partner's splinter shows 16-18, therefore you are in the slam zone. Bid 4NT, Blackwood.

Deal 22

1. No, you do not usually splinter over a minor when you have another logical bid. You should bid 1♡. (Besides, you do not splinter with a singleton ace.)

2. No. You still have a singleton ace. Bid Jacoby 2NT.

Deal 23

1. You are too strong for a splinter: bid 1♠.
2. Bid 4♣, splinter. The double jump would take you to 5♣ — too high — so this is the exception. You have all the qualifications, 13-15 points, a singleton and at least four-card trump support
3. Bid 4NT. You have a great hand and, if partner is interested in slam, you are too.

Deal 24

1. Bid 1♠. With only three trumps, you must not splinter. Show your own suit.
2. Bid 4◊. You have the right qualifications over a spade opening.
3. Bid 1♠. It isn't clear that clubs is the right spot for this hand.
4. Partner knows that you have a singleton or void but does not know that you have a void specifically. Nevertheless you have shown your values and you should not bid again if partner signs off in 4♠.

Deal 25

1. Yes, splinter. Even if partner only has three diamonds, with seven of your own you are pretty sure that diamonds is the right spot. You have enough values for game, lots of trumps and a singleton club.
2. If partner has good diamonds and enough aces you are likely to be able to make slam. You will be quite pleased to continue if partner makes a move to slam.

Deal 26

1. Partner's bid is a splinter. Partner has 18-20 dummy points, enough for game opposite your one-level response. Partner has at least four spades and a singleton diamond.
2. Bid 4♡, a cuebid. You have a terrific hand after partner's splinter. Only the ◊J is wasted and you have 15 high card points opposite partner's big hand. However you cannot bid Blackwood with the low tripleton in clubs.

Deal 27

1 a) Bid 4♠. You have too many wasted diamond points opposite your partner's singleton or void. The ◇K -J-10 may take no tricks at all and are worth little more than three small diamonds.

   b) Bid 4NT. You have an excellent hand opposite partner's heart singleton. If partner has enough aces you should make slam.

   c) Bid 4♠. You do not have enough for slam opposite partner's limit raise.

Deal 28

1. No you should not splinter with only three trumps.

2. Bid 4NT. You have a good fitting hand with only one wasted point in diamonds. You should have enough for slam if partner has enough aces.

Deal 29

1. No. Firstly, A-K-Q is very good but it still doesn't count as four trumps and secondly, you have too many points.

2. It is hard to tell for sure. They may be equal or one might be a bit better. Even if partner has five little spades you may not have a trump loser in spades. If partner has the ◇K and ◇Q then you won't have a diamond loser. We can create hands where spades are better and some where diamonds are better. However, spades are worth more on the score sheet, so we would pick spades.

3. Partner has not shown more than a minimum opening bid since he was forced to bid over 2◇. Partner has five spades and at least three diamonds. You have an excellent fit with partner and enough to push for slam yourself. Bid Blackwood. Partner will assume that diamonds are trumps and will respond accordingly. You could then return to spades.

Deal 30

1. Yes, bid 4♡. You have 13-15 dummy points, a singleton heart and four trumps.

2. Bid 1♠. Even though you have excellent diamonds this may not be the best place to play the hand. Look for a major-suit fit.

Deal 31

1. Bid 4NT. Although you have a lot of wasted cards in clubs, partner is showing 13-15 points and you have 19 high card points. It is hard to visualize a hand where you do not have a play for 6♡ if you are not off two aces. Even if partner has a concentration of points in spades you are likely to have a good play. For example, if partner has

   ♠ A J 9   ♡ A 10 6 3   ◇ Q 5 4 3 2   ♣ 5

   the slam is reasonable.

2. Bid 4NT. You have a big hand with only the ◇J wasted. This is definitely slam territory.

Deal 32

1. Bid 4♠. Although you have two singletons this hand does not qualify for a splinter. You need 13-15 dummy points for a splinter and you do not have them. 4♠ is a preemptive game raise in spades and that is what you have.

2. Bid 1♠. Diamonds may not be the right place to play the hand. Show partner your spade suit.

Deal 33

1. No. You do not have the requirements to open the bidding.

2. Bid 4◇. When partner opens the bidding 1♡ you have a hand worth 13 dummy points. You have the qualifications for a splinter. You won't splinter as a passed hand very often, but this hand is an exception.

3. Bid 2♡. You do not have the qualifications for a splinter in spades. Do remember though that 2♡ is not forcing as you are a passed hand and a passed hand cannot force.

Deal 34

1. Bid 4◇, splinter. You have enough to make game opposite partner's one-level response. You have four trumps and a singleton
diamond.

2. No, you should pass 4♠. You have a good hand, but you have
already shown that to partner.

Deal 35

1. Bid 4♡, assuming that you and your partner have agreed to play
splinters in this situation. This is one of the 'unusual' splinters
which you make after partner overcalls.

2. Yes. Although you do have a maximum, you still meet the requirements for a splinter after a 1♠ opening bid.

Deal 36

1. 4♣, splinter. You meet the requirements for a splinter.

2. 4♣, splinter. You meet the requirements for a splinter in support
of spades too.

3. 4♠ is a slam try; it shows a first-round spade control and denies a
first-round diamond control. You should bid 5♡. You have no
first-round control to show.

Deal 37

1. No. You should not commit to a minor until you have tried to find
a major-suit fit. Bid 1♡.

2. Bid 4NT — all you need to know about now is aces. It definitely
looks like clubs is the right spot — partner doesn't have a major
suit or he would have bid it. With 20 dummy points, you have
enough points for slam once partner has opened the bidding, and
you have first-or second-round control of all the side suits.

Deal 38

1. If partner bids 4◇, your hand gets a lot better because you have no wasted diamond cards, However if partner bids 4♣, your ♣K is not as useful as a card in one of partner's long suits. If partner bids 4♡, your hand definitely worsens. The ♡K and ♡Q will take at least one trick but they are not as valuable as cards in partner's long suit. If you had three little hearts instead, you could still take tricks by ruffing them with partner's trumps.

2. Bid 4♠. This bid has made your hand worse.

Deal 39

1. Bid 4◇, splinter. You only need 16 dummy points to splinter after partner has made a two-over-one response since partner is showing at least 10 points. In this situation you cannot make a double jump because that will take you past the four-level, so you make a single jump to 4◇ to show heart support and the diamond singleton.

2. Partner is showing slam interest and a first-round spade control. Bid 4NT. Your side has first- or second-round controls in all suits and if partner is willing to make a slam move, so are you.

Deal 40

1. No, your hand is too strong. A splinter shows 13-15 points and you have at least 20 dummy points.

2. No. You are too strong to splinter. Bid 4NT. You have a huge hand and you want to be in slam. Just check for aces. This hand is a good candidate for Roman Keycard since you would like to know about the ◇K as well. Roman Keycard Blackwood allows you to check for the king and queen of trumps as well as aces.

Deal 1 - Dealer South

NORTH
♠ K 9 8 7 5
♡ A 9 8 3
◊ 3
♣ K Q 5

□

SOUTH
♠ A Q J 4 2
♡ J 4
◊ K Q 9
♣ J 8 7

NORTH	SOUTH
	1♠
4◊	4♠

Deal 2 - Dealer North

NORTH
♠ A K J
♡ A Q 10 5 4
◊ A 2
♣ 9 8 2

□

SOUTH
♠ Q 10 7 4
♡ K J 8 6
◊ K Q 5 3
♣ 7

NORTH	SOUTH
1♡	4♣
4NT	5♣¹
6♡	

1. One keycard.

Deal 3 - Dealer South

NORTH
♠ J 10 8 7 5
♡ A Q J
♢ K 2
♣ J 5 4

□

SOUTH
♠ A K Q 3
♡ K 10 9
♢ A J 10 9 7
♣ 6

NORTH	SOUTH
	1♢
1♠	4♣
4NT	5♢[1]
6♠	

1. Three keycards.

Deal 4 - Dealer North

NORTH
♠ K J 10 5 2
♡ A 9 5 2
♢ A J
♣ K 3

□

SOUTH
♠ Q 7 6 4
♡ 3
♢ K 7 6 5 2
♣ Q J 5

NORTH	SOUTH
1♠	3♠[1]
4♠	

1. Limit raise

Deal 5 - Dealer South

NORTH
♠ 8
♡ K 7 3 2
♢ K J 9 8
♣ K Q 7 6

□

SOUTH
♠ 3 2
♡ A Q J 10 6 5
♢ A Q 7 6
♣ 5

NORTH	SOUTH
	1♡
3♠	4NT
5♣[1]	5♡

1. 1 keycard

Deal 6 - Dealer North

NORTH
♠ K Q 8 3 2
♡ A 9 8 4
◇ K Q 3
♣ 7

☐

SOUTH
♠ A 4
♡ K Q J 7 5
◇ A 5
♣ A 8 3 2

NORTH	SOUTH
1♠	2♡
4♣	4NT
5♣[1]	5NT
6♡[2]	7♡

1. 1 keycard
2. 2 side kings

Deal 7 - Dealer South

NORTH
♠ 10
♡ A 10 9 8 2
◇ K Q 3
♣ K 7 3 2

☐

SOUTH
♠ Q 9 8
♡ K Q J 7 5
◇ A J 2
♣ J 5

NORTH	SOUTH
	1♡
3♠	4♡

Deal 8 - Dealer North

NORTH
♠ 9 8 7 6 5
♡ A K Q 2
◇ A 2
♣ A 5

☐

SOUTH
♠ A Q J 10
♡ 6 5 4
◇ 7
♣ K Q 10 4 2

NORTH	SOUTH
1♠	4◇
4NT	5♣[1]
6♠	

1. 1 keycard

Deal 9 - Dealer North

NORTH
♠ Q 10 9 8 3
♡ A K J 4 2
◇ 3
♣ 4 5

SOUTH
♠ J 7 6
♡ Q 10 6 5 3
◇ K 9 7
♣ A Q 2

NORTH	SOUTH
1♠	2♡
4◇	4♡

Deal 10 - Dealer North

NORTH
♠ 3
♡ K Q 8 7
◇ A K J 8 5
♣ K J 3

SOUTH
♠ 9 8 4 2
♡ A J 6 3
◇ Q 4
♣ A Q 5

NORTH	SOUTH
1◇	1♡
3♠	4♣
4◇	4NT
5♠[1]	6♡

1. 2 keycards and the trump Q

Deal 11 - Dealer South

NORTH
♠ A K Q 3
♡ J 9 7 5
◇ 3
♣ A K 6 5

SOUTH
♠ J 5 4 2
♡ K 10
◇ A K J 10 9
♣ Q 7

NORTH	SOUTH
	1◇
1♡	1♠
4♠	

Deal 12 - Dealer South

NORTH
♠ 8 7
♡ K Q 4 2
◇ J 10 3
♣ A Q J 4

SOUTH
♠ 4
♡ A J 6 3
◇ A K Q
♣ K 10 6 5 2

NORTH	SOUTH
	1♣
1♡	3♠
4♣	4NT
5♠[1]	6♡

1. 2 keycards and the trump Q

Deal 13 - Dealer North

NORTH
♠ A Q 9 8 5
♡ K J 7
◇ K 7 3 2
♣ 4

SOUTH
♠ K 10 7 4
♡ —
◇ A 9 8 5
♣ K J 9 8 5

NORTH	SOUTH
1♠	4♡
4♠	

Deal 14 - Dealer South

NORTH
♠ A
♡ A 9 8 4
◇ K 10 9 7 6
♣ K 9 2

SOUTH
♠ K J 10 9 8
♡ 3
◇ Q J 8 5 2
♣ A Q

NORTH	SOUTH
	1♠
2◇	4♡
4NT	5♣[1]
6◇	

1. 1 keycard

Deal 15 - Dealer South

NORTH
♠ 6 3
♡ A Q 6 3
◇ A J 9 7 6 3
♣ 3

SOUTH
♠ A K J 9 4
♡ K 10 5 4
◇ K 2
♣ 5 4

NORTH	SOUTH
	1♠
2◇	2♡
4♣	4NT
5♠[1]	6♡

1. 2 keycards and the trump Q

Deal 16 - Dealer North

NORTH
♠ A Q 7 3
♡ Q J 9 4
◇ K 3
♣ J 7 4

SOUTH
♠ K 10 5 4
♡ A K 7 2
◇ 6
♣ K Q 5 2

NORTH	SOUTH
1♣	1♡
2♡	4♣
4♡	4NT
5♣[1]	5♡

1. 1 keycard

Deal 17 - Dealer South

NORTH
♠ Q 10 9 6
♡ 7
◇ K J 5
♣ A Q 10 3 2

SOUTH
♠ A K J 5 4
♡ K J 9
◇ A Q 7 6
♣ 7

NORTH	SOUTH
	1♠
4♡	4NT
5♣[1]	6♠

1. 1 keycard

Deal 18 - Dealer South

NORTH
♠ 6
♡ A K Q 7
◇ K Q 10 5 4
♣ A Q 3

SOUTH
♠ K 3 2
♡ J 10 9 6 5
◇ A 9
♣ K J 10

NORTH	SOUTH
	1♡
4NT	5♣¹
6♡	

1. 1 keycard

Deal 19 - Dealer North

NORTH
♠ Q 9 8 5
♡ A K 7 6
◇ K
♣ K J 5 3

SOUTH
♠ A K J 10 6
♡ 8 2
◇ A Q J 10 2
♣ A

NORTH	SOUTH
	1♠
2NT	4◇
4♡	4NT
5♣¹	5◇²
7♠³	

1. 1 keycard
2. Queen ask
3. Whatever he wants, I have it

Deal 20 - Dealer South

NORTH
♠ K Q 6
♡ Q 6
◇ A 10 7 6 3
♣ J 9 7

SOUTH
♠ A J 3
♡ A J 9 8 5
◇ K Q J 9 2
♣ —

NORTH	SOUTH
	1♡
2◇	4♣
4◇	4♡
4NT	5◇¹
6◇	

1. 3 keycards

Deal 21 - Dealer South

NORTH
♠ A 9 6
♡ K Q 8 7 6 5
◇ 3
♣ A K 9

☐

SOUTH
♠ K J 5 4 3
♡ A J 10 9
◇ A K 4
♣ 6

NORTH	SOUTH
	1♠
2♡	4♣
4NT	5♡[1]
5NT	6♡[2]
7♡	

1. 2 keycards, no trump Q
2. 2 side kings

Deal 22 - Dealer South

NORTH
♠ A
♡ K 10 9 8 7
◇ K Q 5 4 3
♣ 7 6

☐

SOUTH
♠ K J
♡ A Q 5 4 3
◇ J 9
♣ A J 3 2

NORTH	SOUTH
	1♡
2NT	3♡
3♠	4♣
4NT	5♠[1]
6♡	

1. 2 keycards with the trump Q

Deal 23 - Dealer North

NORTH
♠ 8
♡ K J 5 4 3
◇ A K Q J 4
♣ 10 3

☐

SOUTH
♠ A Q J 3 2
♡ A Q
◇ 10 9 8 5 3
♣ 6

NORTH	SOUTH
1♡	1♠
2◇	4♣
4NT	5♡[1]
6◇	

1. 2 keycards, no trump Q

Deal 24 - Dealer North

NORTH
♠ A J 10 5 2
♡ K J
◇ A Q 5 4
♣ 9 2

☐

SOUTH
♠ K 9 6 4 3
♡ Q 10 9
◇ —
♣ A J 10 8 3

NORTH	SOUTH
1♠	4◇
4♠	

Deal 25 - Dealer South

NORTH
♠ K Q 2
♡ A Q
◇ A 9 8 7 6 5 4
♣ 6

☐

SOUTH
♠ A 4
♡ K J 9 8
◇ K Q J 2
♣ 10 5 4

NORTH	SOUTH
	1◇
4♣	4♠
4NT	5♠[1]
6◇	

1. 2 keycards with the trump Q

Deal 26 - Dealer North

NORTH
♠ A Q J 5
♡ K J 8 5
◇ 5
♣ K Q 9 8

☐

SOUTH
♠ K 10 9 3 2
♡ A Q
◇ A J 6
♣ J 7 6

NORTH	SOUTH
1♣	1♠
4◇	4♡
4NT	5◇[1]
6♠	

1. 3 keycards

Deal 27 - Dealer South

NORTH
♠ A 10 3 2
♡ Q 8 6 2
◇ 5
♣ A Q 5 2

SOUTH
♠ K Q 9 5 4
♡ A 5 4 3
◇ K J 10
♣ 10

NORTH	SOUTH
	1♠
4◇	4♠

Deal 28 - Dealer North

NORTH
♠ A K J 5 2
♡ A Q 10
◇ J 4 3 2
♣ 9

SOUTH
♠ Q 9 6 3
♡ K J 5 4
◇ 9
♣ A Q 8 2

NORTH	SOUTH
1♠	4◇
4NT	5♣[1]
6♠	

1. 1 keycard

Deal 29 - Dealer South

NORTH
♠ A K Q
♡ 9
◇ A J 10 5 4
♣ A 6 5 2

SOUTH
♠ J 10 9 8 5
♡ K Q 10
◇ K Q 3 2
♣ K

NORTH	SOUTH
	1♠
2◇	3◇
4NT	5♣[1]
6♠	

1. 1 keycard

Deal 30 - Dealer North

NORTH
♠ A K J 7 5
♡ K 10 5
◇ A 10 2
♣ A 2

☐

SOUTH
♠ Q 9 8 6
♡ 3
◇ K Q J 9 5
♣ K 8 4

NORTH	SOUTH
1♠	4♡
5♣	5♠
6♠	

Deal 31 - Dealer South

NORTH
♠ K 2
♡ A 9 8 7 6
◇ 5
♣ A 10 9 8 5

☐

SOUTH
♠ Q
♡ K Q J 5 2
◇ A J 7
♣ K Q J 3

NORTH	SOUTH
	1♡
4◇	4NT
5♡¹	6♡

1. 2 keycards, no trump Q

Deal 32 - Dealer North

NORTH
♠ K Q J 10 2
♡ A J 9
◇ J 7
♣ K Q J

☐

SOUTH
♠ 9 8 7 6 5 4
♡ 3
◇ K Q 5 4 3
♣ 3

NORTH	SOUTH
1♠	4♠

Deal 33 - Dealer North

NORTH
- ♠ 9 8 7
- ♡ A K 4 3 2
- ◇ 7
- ♣ Q J 10 2

SOUTH
- ♠ A K 3
- ♡ Q J 10 9 5
- ◇ A J 2
- ♣ K 5

NORTH	SOUTH
pass	1♡
4◇	4NT
5♡¹	6♡

1. 2 keycards, no trump Q

Deal 34 - Dealer South

NORTH
- ♠ KQJ3
- ♡ 872
- ◇ KQ5
- ♣ 652

SOUTH
- ♠ A985
- ♡ AQ6
- ◇ 2
- ♣ AK873

NORTH	SOUTH
	1♣
1♠	4◇
4♠	

Deal 35 - Dealer West. West opens 1◇

NORTH
- ♠ KQ1098
- ♡ 76
- ◇ AJ
- ♣ KQ42

SOUTH
- ♠ A754
- ♡ 3
- ◇ K42
- ♣ AJ1076

WEST	NORTH	EAST	SOUTH
1◇	1♠	pass	4♡
pass	4NT	pass	5♡¹
pass	6♠		

1. 2 keycards, no trump Q

Deal 36 - Dealer South

NORTH
♠ K 10 9 5 2
♡ A Q 6 5
◇ Q J 5
♣ 7

SOUTH
♠ A
♡ K J 10 9 8
◇ A K 10 9 8
♣ 5 4

NORTH	SOUTH
	1♡
4♣	4NT
5♣[1]	6♡

1. 1 keycard

Deal 37 - Dealer North

NORTH
♠ Q 9 5
♡ A 6
◇ A J
♣ Q 10 9 8 6 2

SOUTH
♠ K 2
♡ K Q 8 5 4
◇ 6
♣ A K J 5 4

NORTH	SOUTH
1♣	1♡
2♣	4◇
4♡	4NT
5♠[1]	6♣

1. 2 keycards with the trump Q

Deal 38 - Dealer North

NORTH
♠ A Q 9 8 5
♡ K Q 9
◇ 8 3 2
♣ K 2

SOUTH
♠ K J 7 6
♡ 3
◇ A Q 6 5 4
♣ Q 10 3

NORTH	SOUTH
1♠	4♡
4♠	

Deal 39 - Dealer South

NORTH
♠ J 2
♡ A 10 9 5 4
◇ K Q 3
♣ J 9 2

SOUTH
♠ A Q 8 4 3
♡ K Q J 2
◇ 9
♣ K 7 6

NORTH	SOUTH
	1♠
2♡	4◇
4♡	

Deal 40 - Dealer South

NORTH
♠ K Q 10 9 2
♡ 3
◇ A Q 9 8 4
♣ A K

SOUTH
♠ A 6
♡ K Q J 5 4
◇ K Q 7 6
♣ Q 6

NORTH	SOUTH
	1♡
1♠	2◇
4NT	5♠[1]
6◇	

1. 2 keycards with the trump Q

PRACTICE HANDS

Section 6: *Practice Hands* • **51**

Hand 1 - Dealer South

♠ K 9 8 7 5
♡ A 9 8 3
♢ 3
♣ K Q 5

YOUR AUCTION	
NORTH	SOUTH

Hand 2 - Dealer North

♠ A K J
♡ A Q 10 5 4
♢ A 2
♣ 9 8 2

YOUR AUCTION	
NORTH	SOUTH

Hand 3 - Dealer South

♠ J 10 8 7 5
♡ A Q J
♢ K 2
♣ J 5 4

YOUR AUCTION	
NORTH	SOUTH

Hand 4 - Dealer North

♠ K J 10 5 2
♡ A 9 5 2
♢ A J
♣ K 3

YOUR AUCTION	
NORTH	SOUTH

Hand 5 - Dealer South

♠ 8
♡ K 7 3 2
♢ K J 9 8
♣ K Q 7 6

YOUR AUCTION	
NORTH	SOUTH

Hand 6 - Dealer North

♠ K Q 8 3 2
♡ A 9 8 4
◇ K Q 3
♣ 7

YOUR AUCTION	
NORTH	SOUTH

Hand 7 - Dealer South

♠ 10
♡ A 10 9 8 2
◇ K Q 3
♣ K 7 3 2

YOUR AUCTION	
NORTH	SOUTH

Hand 8 - Dealer North

♠ 9 8 7 6 5
♡ A K Q 2
◇ A 2
♣ A 5

YOUR AUCTION	
NORTH	SOUTH

Hand 9 - Dealer North

♠ Q 10 9 8 3
♡ A K J 4 2
◇ 3
♣ K 5

YOUR AUCTION	
NORTH	SOUTH

Hand 10 - Dealer North

♠ 3
♡ K Q 8 7
◇ A K J 8 5
♣ K J 3

YOUR AUCTION	
NORTH	SOUTH

Hand 11 - Dealer South

♠ A K Q 3
♡ J 9 7 5
◇ 3
♣ A K 6 5

YOUR AUCTION	
NORTH	SOUTH

Hand 12 - Dealer South

♠ 8 7
♡ K Q 4 2
◇ J 10 3
♣ A Q J 4

YOUR AUCTION	
NORTH	SOUTH

Hand 13 - Dealer North

♠ A Q 9 8 5
♡ K J 7
◇ K 7 3 2
♣ 4

YOUR AUCTION	
NORTH	SOUTH

Hand 14 - Dealer South

♠ A
♡ A 9 8 4
◇ K 10 9 7 6
♣ K 9 2

YOUR AUCTION	
NORTH	SOUTH

Hand 15 - Dealer South

♠ 6 3
♡ A Q 6 3
◇ A J 9 7 6 3
♣ 3

YOUR AUCTION	
NORTH	SOUTH

Hand 16 - Dealer North

♠ A Q 7 3
♡ Q J 9 4
◇ K 3
♣ J 7 4

YOUR AUCTION

NORTH	SOUTH

Hand 17 - Dealer South

♠ Q 10 9 6
♡ 7
◇ K J 5
♣ A Q 10 3 2

YOUR AUCTION

NORTH	SOUTH

Hand 18 - Dealer South

♠ 6
♡ A K Q 7
◇ K Q 10 5 4
♣ A Q 3

YOUR AUCTION

NORTH	SOUTH

Hand 19 - Dealer North

♠ Q 9 8 5
♡ A K 7 6
◇ K
♣ K J 5 3

YOUR AUCTION

NORTH	SOUTH

Hand 20 - Dealer South

♠ K Q 6
♡ Q 6
◇ A 10 7 6 3
♣ J 9 7

YOUR AUCTION

NORTH	SOUTH

Hand 21 - Dealer South

♠ A 9 6
♡ K Q 8 7 6 5
◇ 3
♣ A K 9

YOUR AUCTION

NORTH	SOUTH

Hand 22 - Dealer South

♠ A
♡ K 10 9 8 7
◇ K Q 5 4 3
♣ 7 6

YOUR AUCTION

NORTH	SOUTH

Hand 23 - Dealer North

♠ 8
♡ K J 5 4 3
◇ A K Q J 4
♣ 10 3

YOUR AUCTION

NORTH	SOUTH

Hand 24 - Dealer North

♠ A J 10 5 2
♡ K J
◇ A Q 5 4
♣ 9 2

YOUR AUCTION

NORTH	SOUTH

Hand 25 - Dealer South

♠ K Q 2
♡ A Q
◇ A 9 8 7 6 5 4
♣ 6

YOUR AUCTION

NORTH	SOUTH

Hand 26 - Dealer North

♠ A Q J 5
♡ K J 8 5
◇ 5
♣ K Q 9 8

YOUR AUCTION

NORTH	SOUTH

Hand 27 - Dealer South

♠ A 10 3 2
♡ Q 8 6 2
◇ 5
♣ A Q 5 2

YOUR AUCTION

NORTH	SOUTH

Hand 28 - Dealer North

♠ A K J 5 2
♡ A Q 10
◇ J 4 3 2
♣ 9

YOUR AUCTION

NORTH	SOUTH

Hand 29 - Dealer South

♠ A K Q
♡ 9
◇ A J 10 5 4
♣ A 6 5 2

YOUR AUCTION

NORTH	SOUTH

Hand 30 - Dealer North

♠ A K J 7 5
♡ K 10 5
◇ A 10 2
♣ A 2

YOUR AUCTION

NORTH	SOUTH

Hand 31 - Dealer South

♠ K 2
♡ A 9 8 7 6
◊ 5
♣ A 10 9 8 5

YOUR AUCTION

NORTH	SOUTH

Hand 32 - Dealer North

♠ K Q J 10 2
♡ A J 9
◊ J 7
♣ K Q J

YOUR AUCTION

NORTH	SOUTH

Hand 33 - Dealer North

♠ 9 8 7
♡ A K 4 3 2
◊ 7
♣ Q J 10 2

YOUR AUCTION

NORTH	SOUTH

Hand 34 - Dealer South

♠ K Q J 3
♡ 8 7 2
◊ K Q 5
♣ 6 5 2

YOUR AUCTION

NORTH	SOUTH

Hand 35 - Dealer West opens 1◊

♠ K Q 10 9 8
♡ 7 6
◊ A J
♣ K Q 4 2

YOUR AUCTION

NORTH	SOUTH

Hand 36 - Dealer South

♠ K 10 9 5 2
♡ A Q 6 5
♢ Q J 5
♣ 7

YOUR AUCTION

NORTH   SOUTH

Hand 37 - Dealer North

♠ Q 9 5
♡ A 6
♢ A J
♣ Q 10 9 8 6 2

YOUR AUCTION

NORTH   SOUTH

Hand 38 - Dealer North

♠ A Q 9 8 5
♡ K Q 9
♢ 8 3 2
♣ K 2

YOUR AUCTION

NORTH   SOUTH

Hand 39 - Dealer South

♠ J 2
♡ A 10 9 5 4
♢ K Q 3
♣ J 9 2

YOUR AUCTION

NORTH   SOUTH

Hand 40 - Dealer South

♠ K Q 10 9 2
♡ 3
♢ A Q 9 8 4
♣ A K

YOUR AUCTION

NORTH   SOUTH

Hand 1 - Dealer South

♠ A Q J 4 2
♡ J 4
◇ K Q 9
♣ J 8 7

YOUR AUCTION

NORTH	SOUTH

Hand 2 - Dealer North

♠ Q 10 7 4
♡ K J 8 6
◇ K Q 5 3
♣ 7

YOUR AUCTION

NORTH	SOUTH

Hand 3 - Dealer South

♠ A K Q 3
♡ K 10 9
◇ A J 10 9 7
♣ 6

YOUR AUCTION

NORTH	SOUTH

Hand 4 - Dealer North

♠ Q 7 6 4
♡ 3
◇ K 7 6 5 2
♣ Q J 5

YOUR AUCTION

NORTH	SOUTH

Hand 5 - Dealer South

♠ 3 2
♡ A Q J 10 6 5
◇ A Q 7 6
♣ 5

YOUR AUCTION

NORTH	SOUTH

Hand 6 - Dealer North

♠ A 4
♡ K Q J 7 5
◇ A 5
♣ A 8 3 2

YOUR AUCTION

NORTH	SOUTH

Hand 7 - Dealer South

♠ Q 9 8
♡ K Q J 7 5
◇ A J 2
♣ J 5

YOUR AUCTION

NORTH	SOUTH

Hand 8 - Dealer North

♠ A Q J 10
♡ 6 5 4
◇ 7
♣ K Q 10 4 2

YOUR AUCTION

NORTH	SOUTH

Hand 9 - Dealer North

♠ J 7 6
♡ Q 10 6 5 3
◇ K 9 7
♣ A Q 2

YOUR AUCTION

NORTH	SOUTH

Hand 10 - Dealer North

♠ 9 8 4 2
♡ A J 6 3
◇ Q 4
♣ A Q 5

YOUR AUCTION

NORTH	SOUTH

Hand 11 - Dealer South

♠ J 5 4 2
♡ K 10
◇ A K J 10 9
♣ Q 7

YOUR AUCTION

NORTH	SOUTH

Hand 12 - Dealer South

♠ 4
♡ A J 6 3
◇ A K Q
♣ K 10 6 5 2

YOUR AUCTION

NORTH	SOUTH

Hand 13 - Dealer North

♠ K 10 7 4
♡ —
◇ A 9 8 5
♣ K J 9 8 5

YOUR AUCTION

NORTH	SOUTH

Hand 14 - Dealer South

♠ K J 10 9 8
♡ 3
◇ Q J 8 5 2
♣ A Q

YOUR AUCTION

NORTH	SOUTH

Hand 15 - Dealer South

♠ A K J 9 4
♡ K 10 5 4
◇ K 2
♣ 5 4

YOUR AUCTION

NORTH	SOUTH

Hand 16 - Dealer North

♠ K 10 5 4
♡ A K 7 2
◇ 6
♣ K Q 5 2

YOUR AUCTION	
NORTH	SOUTH

Hand 17 - Dealer South

♠ A K J 5 4
♡ K J 9
◇ A Q 7 6
♣ 7

YOUR AUCTION	
NORTH	SOUTH

Hand 18 - Dealer South

♠ K 3 2
♡ J 10 9 6 5
◇ A 9
♣ K J 10

YOUR AUCTION	
NORTH	SOUTH

Hand 19 - Dealer North

♠ A K J 10 6
♡ 8 2
◇ A Q J 10 2
♣ A

YOUR AUCTION	
NORTH	SOUTH

Hand 20 - Dealer South

♠ A J 3
♡ A J 9 8 5
◇ K Q J 9 2
♣ —

YOUR AUCTION	
NORTH	SOUTH

Hand 21 - Dealer South

♠ K J 5 4 3
♡ A J 10 9
◇ A K 4
♣ 6

YOUR AUCTION

NORTH	SOUTH

Hand 22 - Dealer South

♠ K J
♡ A Q 5 4 3
◇ J 9
♣ A J 3 2

YOUR AUCTION

NORTH	SOUTH

Hand 23 - Dealer North

♠ A Q J 3 2
♡ A Q
◇ 10 9 8 5 3
♣ 6

YOUR AUCTION

NORTH	SOUTH

Hand 24 - Dealer North

♠ K 9 6 4 3
♡ Q 10 9
◇ —
♣ A J 10 8 3

YOUR AUCTION

NORTH	SOUTH

Hand 25 - Dealer South

♠ A 4
♡ K J 9 8
◇ K Q J 2
♣ 10 5 4

YOUR AUCTION

NORTH	SOUTH

Hand 26 - Dealer North

♠ K 10 9 3 2
♡ A Q
◇ A J 6
♣ J 7 6

YOUR AUCTION

NORTH	SOUTH

Hand 27 - Dealer South

♠ K Q 9 5 4
♡ A 5 4 3
◇ K J 10
♣ 10

YOUR AUCTION

NORTH	SOUTH

Hand 28 - Dealer North

♠ Q 9 6 3
♡ K J 5 4
◇ 9
♣ A Q 8 2

YOUR AUCTION

NORTH	SOUTH

Hand 29 - Dealer South

♠ J 10 9 8 5
♡ K Q 10
◇ K Q 3 2
♣ K

YOUR AUCTION

NORTH	SOUTH

Hand 30 - Dealer North

♠ Q 9 8 6
♡ 3
◇ K Q J 9 5
♣ K 8 4

YOUR AUCTION

NORTH	SOUTH

Hand 31 - Dealer South

♠ Q
♡ K Q J 5 2
◇ A J 7
♣ K Q J 3

YOUR AUCTION	
NORTH	SOUTH

Hand 32 - Dealer North

♠ 9 8 7 6 5 4
♡ 3
◇ K Q 5 4 3
♣ 3

YOUR AUCTION	
NORTH	SOUTH

Hand 33 - Dealer North

♠ A K 3
♡ Q J 10 9 5
◇ A J 2
♣ K 5

YOUR AUCTION	
NORTH	SOUTH

Hand 34 - Dealer South

♠ A 9 8 5
♡ A Q 6
◇ 2
♣ A K 8 7 3

YOUR AUCTION	
NORTH	SOUTH

Hand 35 - Dealer West opens 1◇

♠ A 7 5 4
♡ 3
◇ K 4 2
♣ A J 10 7 6

YOUR AUCTION	
NORTH	SOUTH

Hand 36 - Dealer South

♠ A
♡ K J 10 9 8
◇ A K 10 9 8
♣ 5 4

YOUR AUCTION

NORTH	SOUTH

Hand 37 - Dealer North

♠ K 2
♡ K Q 8 5 4
◇ 6
♣ A K J 5 4

YOUR AUCTION

NORTH	SOUTH

Hand 38 - Dealer North

♠ K J 7 6
♡ 3
◇ A Q 6 5 4
♣ Q 10 3

YOUR AUCTION

NORTH	SOUTH

Hand 39 - Dealer South

♠ A Q 8 4 3
♡ K Q J 2
◇ 9
♣ K 7 6

YOUR AUCTION

NORTH	SOUTH

Hand 40 - Dealer North

♠ A 6
♡ K Q J 5 4
◇ K Q 7 6
♣ Q 6

YOUR AUCTION

NORTH	SOUTH